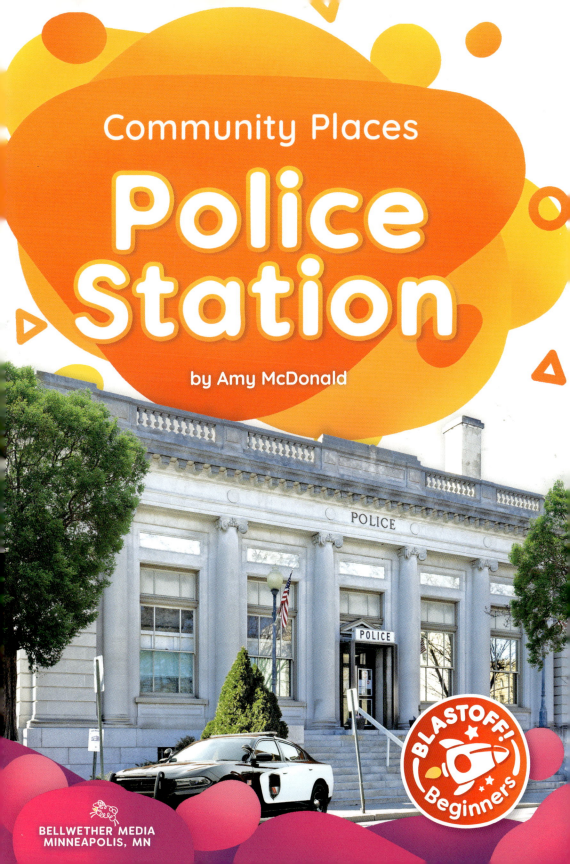

Community Places

Police Station

by Amy McDonald

BLASTOFF! Beginners

BELLWETHER MEDIA
MINNEAPOLIS, MN

Blastoff! Beginners are developed by literacy experts and educators to meet the needs of early readers. These engaging informational texts support young children as they begin reading about their world. Through simple language and high frequency words paired with crisp, colorful photos, Blastoff! Beginners launch young readers into the universe of independent reading.

Sight Words in This Book

a	in	people	to
an	is	she	
are	make	the	
at	many	these	
go	my	they	
help	on	this	

This edition first published in 2022 by Bellwether Media, Inc.

No part of this publication may be reproduced in whole or in part without written permission of the publisher. For information regarding permission, write to Bellwether Media, Inc., Attention: Permissions Department, 6012 Blue Circle Drive, Minnetonka, MN 55343.

Library of Congress Cataloging-in-Publication Data

Names: McDonald, Amy, 1985- author.
Title: Police station / by Amy McDonald.
Description: Minneapolis, MN : Bellwether Media, Inc., 2022. | Series: Blastoff! Beginners : community places | Includes bibliographical references and index. | Audience: Ages PreK-2 | Audience: Grades K-1
Identifiers: LCCN 2021044378 (print) | LCCN 2021044379 (ebook) | ISBN 9781644875681 (library binding) | ISBN 9781648346590 (paperback) | ISBN 9781648345791 (ebook)
Subjects: LCSH: Police--Juvenile literature. | Police stations--Juvenile literature.
Classification: LCC HV7922 .M3745 2022 (print) | LCC HV7922 (ebook) | DDC 363.2--dc23
LC record available at https://lccn.loc.gov/2021044378
LC ebook record available at https://lccn.loc.gov/2021044379

Text copyright © 2022 by Bellwether Media, Inc. BLASTOFF! BEGINNERS and associated logos are trademarks and/or registered trademarks of Bellwether Media, Inc.

Editor: Christina Leaf   Designer: Andrea Schneider

Printed in the United States of America, North Mankato, MN.

Table of Contents

At the Police Station!	4
What Are Police Stations?	6
Working at the Station	10
Police Station Facts	22
Glossary	23
To Learn More	24
Index	24

At the Police Station!

My mom is a police officer. She works at the police station!

police officer

What Are Police Stations?

Police stations are busy places. Everyone is ready to help.

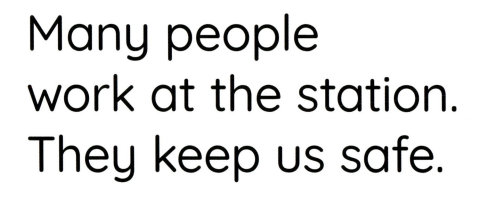

Many people work at the station. They keep us safe.

Working at the Station

This is a meeting room. Officers make plans.

meeting room

This is a cell. Officers bring in **suspects**.

cell

This is a lab. They take **fingerprints**.

fingerprints

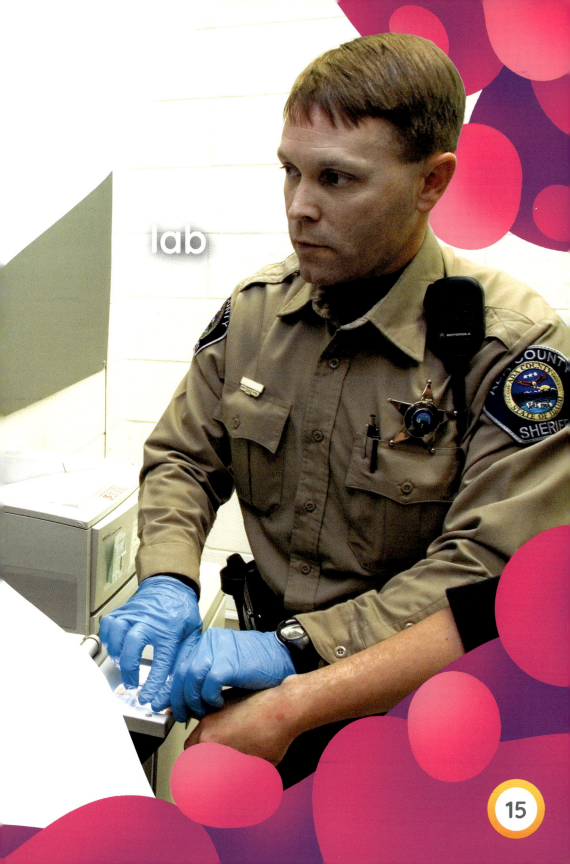

This is an office. **Detectives** work on **cases**.

case folders

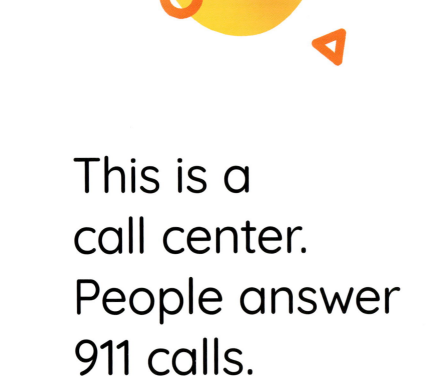

This is a call center. People answer 911 calls.

call center

These are police cars. Officers go to help!

police car

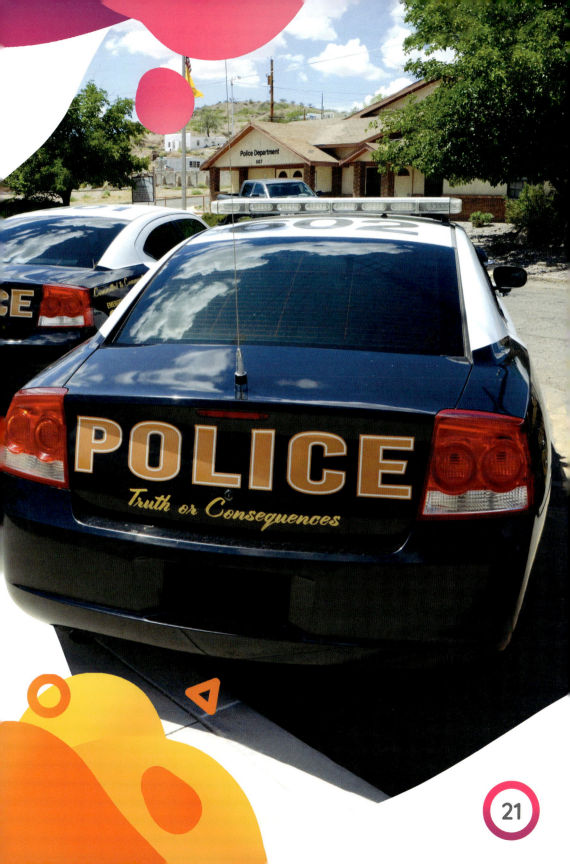

Police Station Facts

Inside a Police Station

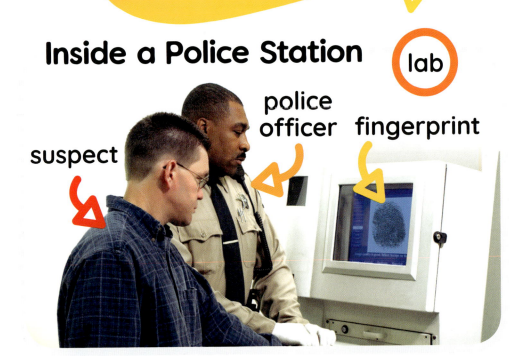

suspect | police officer | fingerprint | lab

What Happens in a Police Station?

bring in suspects | take fingerprints | answer 911 calls

Glossary

cases

problems that detectives and officers work on

detectives

people who use clues to find out what happened

fingerprints

marks made by fingertips

suspects

people who may have done crimes

To Learn More

ON THE WEB

FACTSURFER

Factsurfer.com gives you a safe, fun way to find more information.

1. Go to www.factsurfer.com.
2. Enter "police station" into the search box and click 🔍.
3. Select your book cover to see a list of related content.

Index

911 calls, 18
call center, 18, 19
cases, 16
cell, 12
detectives, 16, 17
fingerprints, 14
help, 6, 20
lab, 14, 15
meeting room, 10, 11
office, 16
plans, 10
police cars, 20
police officer, 4, 5, 10, 12, 20
safe, 8
suspects, 12, 13
works, 4, 8, 16

The images in this book are reproduced through the courtesy of: Brian Logan Photography, front cover (station); Fiat Chrysler Automotive, front cover (police car), p. 20; LifetimeStock, p. 3; kali9, pp. 4-5; Eddie Gerald/ Alamy, pp. 6-7; Sean Locke Photography, p. 8; SDI Productions, pp. 8-9; Jeffrey Isaac Greenberg 5+/ Alamy, pp. 10-11; Thomas Imo/ Getty Images, p. 12 (cell); Daxus, pp. 12-13; Andrey_Kuzmin, p. 14; David R. Frazier Photolibrary/ Alamy, pp. 14-15; rilence, p. 16; miodrag ignjatovic, pp. 16-17; ZUMA Press/ Alamy, pp. 18-19; simon leigh/ Alamy, pp. 20-21; Thinkstock/ Getty Images, p. 22 (inside); Mark Harvey/ Alamy, p. 22 (bring in suspects); Goads Agency, p. 22 (take fingerprints); knyazevfoto, p. 22 (answer 911 calls); Peter Casolino/ Alamy, p. 23 (cases); Photographee.eu, p. 23 (detectives); Bushko Oleksandr, p. 23 (fingerprints); Lisa F. Young, p. 23 (suspects).